The Power of Allahs 99 Names

In your heart

A guide for the daily recitation

for purification

C. K.

Imprint

Text:	04/2020© Copyright by Cigdem K.
Cover:	04/2020© Copyright by Cigdem K.
ISBN	978-3-347-06070-8 (e-Book)
Publisher:	Tredition GmbH Halenreie 40-44 22359 Hamburg

„God has the lovely names. Call him within those.

Don´t listen to those, who denies Allah's Names "

(Al´Araf (Sure 7), 180.Ayat (Verse))

"I am close to my servants; I am closer to them than their inner carotid artery.

Whenever they turn towards me and worship me, I will listen and answer their prayers "

(Al-Baqara Sure, 186. Ayat (Verse))

Table of content

Legal instructions: 2

Preface 1

The purification 3

Esma Ul Husna 33

Abundance 110

Recitation Examples in Practice 112

Recitation for „On the Go" 116

Prayers for Forgiveness and Healing 118

The Prayer of Hızır in Hıdırellez 120

The Intention 127

Preface

Throughout the world, people recite certain phrases in everyday life (also called "affirmations"), such as "I can do this" or "I am valuable". Other people apply the so-called mantra meditation, where one focuses all one's attention on certain affirmations, with the mind slowly deviating. In mantra meditation, the words do not need to have any real meaning; they are merely a tool to achieve the state of meditation. Whereas Allah and all His beautiful names (Esma Úl-Húsna) have meaning and are very powerful.

In this book, I would like to introduce the 99 Names of Allah and their effect on us when we recite them regularly. We get into a state of meditation and through that we can let these names into our heart. We let Allah into our heart. In practice, in order to achieve the state of meditation and to have a particularly powerful effect, certain prayers should be recited and purification should be performed before each recitation. In this book, I would like to offer instructions for daily recitation that can be performed any-time and anywhere. Allah has no particular place, because Allah is everywhere.

Everything in the world is a test, everything good and everything bad that befalls us and that exists.

Allah keeps the world in balance as well as in imbalance. Sometimes the good prevails and sometimes the bad. Sometimes goodness reigns and sometimes badness reigns. Sometimes there is much injustice and many diseases and sometimes there is justice, love and happiness. It is all at the discretion of Allah. Allah knows the hidden and the visible. Even if we do not always understand everything, we must always trust in Allah.

This imbalance and balance will always increase and decrease until the day we have to give an account. Allah always encourages us to turn to Him and ask Him for everything we need and desire, at any time, through the recitation of all His names known to us.

It is recommended to do a "Niyyah" (intention) before starting to recite Allah´s names. For instance, to open your hands and pray to Allah about things you want to have in your life, material and immaterial such as success, healthiness, happiness or love. Then start with reciting the esma, which supports your "Niyyah".

The purification

Purification has a high significance in Islam. Not only the spiritual purification through prayer and recitation, but also the physical cleansing before the recitation and the cleansing of the environment where the prayer and recitation are carried out. The entire home must always be clean and on the floor should not be dirt or dust from street shoes or something similar.

In Islam, it is believed that the disorder in the apartment (as well as dirt and dust) releases negative energies and affects the prayer or recitation. Therefore, the apartment should always be aired and clean.

"If my servants turn to me and worship me, I will answer their prayers..."

(Al-Baqara Surah, 186th Ayat (verse))

The Daily Recitation

By practicing the so-called "Dhikr" (repetitive recitation of the names of Allah in a kind of meditation) on a daily or weekly basis, your attitude towards certain challenges in everyday life will change and you will react more confidently, more assertively and more peacefully. Because there is someone watching over you at all times and this certainty will bring you security and you will start to let go.

It also helps with mental and health discomfort. Of course, this is not to be considered a substitute for a medication. This is about spiritual purification.

If you are carrying a lot of emotional baggage, it can make you sick in the long-term. This reflects on your health and you get physical discomfort. This needs to be purified on a regular basis.

You can imagine it like as follows: Every year in spring we clean the house, clean behind the furniture, replace broken or old things. Just like this annual cleaning, our soul also needs a regular cleansing in order to throw off emotional ballast by forgiving as well as asking for forgiveness and turning to God.

For a daily recitation, gemstones are also suitable, you can either make a prayer wreath from them or hold the stones in your hands during the recitation. Afterwards you can carry them with you so that they give off the positive energy.

Suitable for this purpose are tourmaline, quartz, jade, turquoise stones, ametiste, as well as rock crystals, emeralds, pearls, tiger's eye, charoite, hematite (and others).

"When My servant comes striding toward Me, I come hastening to him."

[Sahih Muslim, Hadithnr. 4832/Chapter 48]

Recitation duration

In practice, just 10-15 minutes a day is sufficient to feel a change. Recitation can be done at any time of day, anytime, anywhere.

However, recitation immediately after morning prayer (Fajr) as well as after night prayer (Isha) or at night is particularly effective for most names. I will describe in this book the frequency, time and duration of each name for curative recitation.

Whenever you are not feeling well, whenever you are at a loss, feel lonely or have mental or physical complaints:

Turn to Allah and recite the 99 most beautiful names.

Curative Prayers

When we do not feel well, are troubled by inner turmoil or are in a difficult situation with many problems, these prayers help. They give positive energy. We ask Allah here for material as well as ideal things in life and in the hereafter:

„Rabbenâ âtinâ fi'd-duunyâ haseneten ve fi'lâhirati haseneten. Ve kınâ ʿazâbe'n-nâr"

„Rabbena'ğfirlî ve li vâlideyye ve lil mu'minîne yevme yekûmu'l-hisâb"

„Allahumme salli ala seyyidina Muhammedin tibbiˊl-kulubi ve devaiha ve afiyetiˊl-ebdani ve Şifaiha ve nuriˊl -ebsari ve diyaiha ve ala alihi ve sahbihi ve sellim"

There are several ayat (verses) in the Quran that are said to provide healing (physical and spiritual). The recitation of certain suras also promises healing and supports the faster fulfillment of prayers.

Surah Al-Kawthar "The abundance"

Bismillahirrahmanirrahim

İnna a'taynakel kevser. Fesalli li rabbike venhar. İnne şanieke huuvel'ebter.

"Indeed, We have granted you ˹O Prophet˺ abundant goodness. So pray and sacrifice to your Lord ˹alone. Only the one who hates you is truly cut off ˹from any goodness."

„Estagfurullah"

Practice: 33 times before bedtime or after the night prayer, this recitation promises healing in conjunction with the protective prayers, the suras from the Qur'an. „Estagfurullah" roughly translated means:

"I ask Allah for forgiveness and for support".

For daily recitation (as well as before the start of recitation), the following suras are suitable:

Fatiha Surah 21 times
Al-Ichlas Surah 7 times
Nas Surah 7 times
Falaq Surah 7 times
Ash-Sharh Surah 21 times
Al Qalam Surah 7 times

According to traditions, our Prophet Hz. Muhammad (sallallahu 'alayhi wa sallam, SAW, meaning: eace be upon him) used to read the surahs Al-Fatiha, En-Nas, Al-Falaq, and Ichlas 7 times into his outstretched hands every night before falling asleep and then rub them over his face and upper body for a restful sleep and protection during sleep. In Al-Baqarah Surah, there is a verse which is the most exalted verse among the Quranic verses. This is the "Âyat-al Kursi." There are hadiths that emphasize the importance of this ayat (verse). In this verse, Allah is described.

Especially when you have inner restlessness, anxiety or when you feel that things are not going well in life, you can recite the following:

Yunus Sure, 81. Ayat (Vers) 33 Mal wiederholen

Ayat Al-Kursi (Al-Baqara, 255. Ayat (Verse) repetition of 7 times (or more)

Al Fatiha Sure, repetition of 21 times

In shā' Allāh (with Allah's will) it will bring you purification and cure.

„if you do not get back the appreciation you give to your counter-
part then break up this frienship"

(the words of prophet Muhammad, sallallahu 'alayhi wa sallam,
SAW, meaning: peace be upon him)

Forgiveness and letting go

We are a small part of a larger whole and have someone (Allah) who guards us, protects us, and gives us what we need, though not always what we desire. Whenever we turn to Allah and pray, we will be heard, and Allah will respond to our prayer. We need to understand that we are protected and everything that happens to us should occur to give us a message:

1. to teach us something (find out what you need to learn),

2. to prepare us for something that is yet to come (a major challenge) or opportunity, a change)

3. or to warn us that we are on the wrong path or that the current situation is not beneficial to us (e.g., Allah wants us to direct our prayers and desires only to Him and not pay more attention to worldly things than necessary)

We must accept everything that happens to us and accept it as a test.

It is important that we forgive all those who have hurt or harmed us in the past or in the present.

Forgiveness is very important for the effect of the recitation.

When we forgive, we let go, and when we let go, we cleanse our heart of all the emotional baggage that we have carried with us for far too long. Only when our heart is clean of emotional baggage can we let Allah into our heart.

"The virtues and secrets of Yunus Surah preserve their youth and freshness, and even the best is the Almighty God. For this reason, the virtues and characteristics of the Quran are stated in verses and hadiths as follows: "This is a great book. We have taken it down. It is very blessed. (Its benefits and abundance are many.) Now obey it, keep its commands, and fear Allah. That mercy may be shown to you. "

(surah Al An´Am, 6/155).

"There are seven verses in which anyone who recites them or carries them with himself, in any case, even if the sky is covered over the earth, Allah will surely provide an exit and salvation for that person (Ali ibn Abi Talib)

(Ali ibn Abi Talib was a cousin and son-in-law of the Islamic prophet Muhammad, who ruled as the fourth caliph from 656 until his assassination in 661)

1. Surah at-Tawbah (51st verse),

2. Surah Yunus (107th verse),

3. Surah Hud (6th verse).

4. Surah Hud (56th verse)

5. Surah al-Ankabut (60th verse),

6. Surah al-Fath (2nd verse)

7. Surah az Zumar (38th verse)"

To purify mental discomfort and negative energy, recite many times (100 times or more – around 15 minutes):

Yunus Surah, 57th Ayat (Verses)

„Ya eyyuhennasu gad caa etkum mev´izatum mirrabbikum ve Şifa ul lima fissuduri ve hudev ve rahmetul lilmu´miniin"

Rough translation

"O mankind! Now there has come to you from your Lord an exhortation, and a healing for that which troubles you (in your hearts), and a guidance and mercy for the faithful."

Yunus Surah, 80th, 81st, 82nd Ayat (Verses)

Eûzu billahi mineş-şeytânirracîm. Bismillahirrahmanirrahîm.

80th: Fe lemmâ elkav kâle mûsâ mâ ci'tum bihis sihr(sihru), innallâhe se yubtiluhu, innallâhe lâ yuslihu amelel mufsidîn

"When the magicians came, Moses said to them, "Cast whatever you wish to cast!"

81st: Ve yuhikkullâhul hakka bi kelimâtihî ve lev kerihel mucrimûn.

"When they did, Moses said, "What you have produced is mere magic, Allah will surely make it useless, for Allah certainly does not set right the work of the corruptors."

82nd: Fe vakaal hakku ve batale mâ kânû ya'melûn(ya'melûne).

"And Allah establishes the truth by His Words—

even to the dismay of the wicked."

Curative ayat

Before we start reciting these following ayat (verse),

we should recite the name of Allah, which we do not find among the 99 names, but can find in the Quran, "Ya Ṣafi," and following it with "Sadiqallahu'l azim" to conclude the prayer. First: Ya Ṣafi, then the following ayat (verse) (can be repeated as many times as desired):

1. At-Tauba(Tawba) Surah, 14th Ayat (Verse), sadiqallahu´l azim

2. Yunus Surah, 57th Ayat (Verse), sadiqallahu´l azim

3. Yunus Surah 81st Ayat (Verse), sadiqallahu´l azim

4. En-Nahl Surah, 69th Ayat (Verse), sadiqallahu´l azim

5. Isra Sure, 82nd Ayat (Verse) sadiqallahu´l azim

6. As-Suara Surah, 80th Ayat (Verse), sadiqallahu´l azim

7. Al-Baqara Surah, 255. Ayat (Verse)

    (Ayat´a- Kursi "Throne Verse")

„Amin"

As-Sarh/ Ash-Sharh Surah: The opening

This surah brings positive energy and resolves various discomforts. It is seen as a curative prayer.

Bismillahirrahmânirrahîm.

1- Elem neşrah leke sadrek

2- Ve vada'na 'anke vizreke

3- Elleziy enkada zahreke

4- Ve refa'na leke zikreke

5- Feinne me'al'usri yuusren

6- İnne me'al'usri yuusren

7- Feiza ferağte fensab

8- Ve ila rabbike ferğab

Rough translation: "In the name of Allah, the All-merciful, the Merciful. Have we not opened and enlarged thy heart. And relieved thee of thy burden. Which made thee crooked and pressed thee down. And increased your prestige? Certainly, with every aggravation comes relief. Now when thou art done (with one task) then exert thyself (for the next task). And direct thy desire toward thy Lord."

In shā' Allāh it will bring you healing.

"I am neither in heaven nor am I on earth... I do not fit any-where...

Except in the hearts of my faithful servants."

(İmam Gazali, book: İhyâ-u Ulûmiddîn)

In shā' Allāh (With Allah's Will) you will find peace!

Preparation for the recitation

Step 1: before the recitation, it is necessary to perform the Islamic ritual cleansing (washing). This cleansing (washing) leads to purification and only then can we stand in front of Allah.

Practice: Recite the following in a low voice (whispering): „Eshhedu en la ilahe illallah ve eshhedu enne Muhammeden rasulullah "

Translation:

"I testify that there is no God but Allah and I testify that Muhammad is Allah's messenger."

while washing the hands 3 times up to the elbow joint, then gargling the mouth with water 3 times and washing the face and feet 3 times each up to the ankle joint while repeating the so-called Shahada each time. In some situations, it is necessary to wash from head to toe and gargle with water three times, and also to draw water through the nose while reciting the Shahada (in any mosque you can find out about the detailed process of washing for different situations). If one does not regularly perform the daily 5 obligatory prayers (namaz), one should recite the following prayers before starting reciting the Names of Allah:

Step 2: It is particularly effective that at least 1 time (or more) a day (optimally) before each recitation to recite following prayers (in low voice; whispering):

Al-Fatiha Surah

al-Ihlās Surah

Nas Surah

Falaq Surah

This makes the recitation particularly effective and protects the positive energies during the recitation. I will present these protective prayers in the next pages.

Al-Fatiha:

This is the first and opening surah from the Quran and means "The Opening"

1- Bismillahirrahmânirrahîm.

2- Elhamduu lillâhi rabbil'alemin

3- Errahmânir'rahim

4- Mâliki yevmiddin

5- İyyâke na'budû ve iyyâke neste'în

6- İhdinessırâtel muustakîm

7- Sırâtellezine en'amte aleyhim ğayrilmağdûbi aleyhim ve leddâllîn

Amin!

"In the name of Allah, the All-Merciful. All praise is due to Allah, the Lord of the Worlds. The Most Merciful, the Most Compassionate. The only Royal Highness on the Day of Judgment. To Thee alone do we serve and to Thee alone do we implore help. Guide us along the straight path. The way of those to whom You have shown Your favor. Not of those who have only won Your wrath. And not of those who go astray. Amin"

Al-Ichlās

Al-Ichlas is the 112th sura of the Qur'an (The Sincerity) and one of the shortest. The U and A are elongated if there is an apostrophe as in the example below.

Bismillahirrahmânirrahîm.

1- Kul hûvallâhû ehad

2- Allâhûssamed

3- Lem yelid ve lem yûled

4- Ve lem yekún lehû kûfûven ehad

"In the name of Allah, the All-merciful, the Merciful. Allah is unique, Allah is eternally Pure. Has not begotten and has not been begotten. And nothing is equal to Allah (Allah is comparable to nothing that exist – Allah has created everything that exist).

Al Falaq

Al-Falaq is the 113th sura of the Qur'an (The Dawn).

Bismillahirrahmânirrahîm.

1- Kul eûzu birabbilfalak.

2- Min şerri mâ halak. (pronounced: sherrii; maa,)

3- Ve min şerri ğâzikin izâ vekab. (soft G= ğ, pronounced in the throat/simpler: long a)

4- Ve min şerri nneffâsâti fil'ukad.

5- Ve min şerri hâsidin izâ hased

"In the name of Allah, the All-merciful, the Merciful. I seek my refuge with the Lord of the Dawn. From the evil of what Allah has created. And from the evil of darkness when it falls. And from the evil of the knot blowers. And from the evil of every envious one when he envies."

An-Nas

An-Nas is the concluding sura in the Quran (Mankind)

Bismillahirrahmânirrahîm.

1- Kul e'ûzuu birabbinnâs

2- Melikinnâs

3- İlâhinnâs

4- Min şerrilvesvâsilhannâs

5- Ellezî yuuvesvisû fî sudûrinnâs

6- Minelcinneti vennâs

"In the name of Allah, the All-Merciful, the Merciful. I seek refuge with the Lord of men. With the King of men. With the God of men. From the evil of the whisperer who escapes (from us) and returns. Who whispers (into the heart) of men. Among the jinn and the people (whom Allah has created).

The Gratitude (Alhamdullillah)

The Curative Effect of the Praises of Allah

Gratitude is very important and should become a part of our daily recitation, repeating the name "Alhamdulillah" daily will purify you and will be the first step to make your wishes come true.

We should always express our gratitude for what we have, for our health, our job, our marriage, our children, our talents and for everything else for which we are grateful. We can also be grateful daily for little things, like the sun shining, getting work done a little earlier than expected, or not having to stand in a traffic jam. Our energy will change for the better and we will feel inner peace.

„Alhamdulillah" الحمد لله

Recitation: 33 times after the morning prayer (Fajr) or after the night prayer. A common translation is:

"My praise and worship to the Lord"

It is common and effective to recite "Alhamdulillah" after eating and drinking (to express gratitude for the food).

The Praise

„Subhanallah" سبحان الله

Recitation: 33 times before bedtime or after night prayer. Subhanallah is often translated as "Glory to God". Alhamdullillah can
also be recited together with "Subhanallah" and with "Allah".

„Bismillahirrahmanirrahim"

بسم الله الرحمن الرحيم

Rough translation:
"In the name of the merciful and gracious God" and contains 2 of
Allah's 99 names, namely "Ar-Rahman" and "Ar-Rahim" at the
end of the word. These names represent health, prosperity and
positive energies. It is an Arabic invocation that is found at the
beginning of every surah of the Quran with one exception.

The miracles of reciting Bismillahirrahmanirrahim in everyday life:

Before bedtime ensures a peaceful sleep
As a recitation 33 times for inner peace
As recitation 786 times for "purification" and increase of own positive energy
As recitation 1000 times for solving problems and blockages
In connection with other names of Allah as recitation (example: "Bismillahil-Latif")
Before eating and drinking
When entering a home for positive energies
When leaving the house protected on the journey
When moving to a new apartment for positive energies
Before each reading of a sura from the Koran
Before every prayer to Allah
When closing doors for positive energies
And much more

In shā' Allāh (With Allah's Will) your prayers will be answered

"In the name of Allah the All-Merciful, the Merciful"

"Verily, Allah was merciful to the believers, since He raised up among them a messenger from among you to recite His verses to them and purify them therewith..."

(Al-Imran Surah, verse 164/ Translation from the book of Sahih Al Buhary).

Esma Ul Husna

Esma-uul Huusna means Allah's beautiful names (and facets) In Arabic "asma Allah al-husna".

In Islam, each of these names represents a characteristic of Allah. Together, these are called the 99 names (Esma) of Allah. They occur in the Koran and are understood as synonyms for Allah.

However, according to traditions, there are many more names and facets of Allah, but we humans are not yet aware of them.

In the Koran there are a few more names that are not known among the 99 names, such as the name Şafi (pronounced:Shaafi, means the healing, this Esma stands for healing). The Esma Şafi is often recited in conjunction with other suras from the Quran for the healing of diseases.

Example: recite „ya Şafi" and surah Al-Kawthar at least 21 times in front of a glass water and then drink it until $1/10^{th}$ remains in the bottom, then water with it plant (e.g. flowers in your home) or pour it into the soil.

When reciting the 99 Esma's of Allah, if the addition of "celle cellaluhu" is added and "Ya" is added before the Esma (attribute), it enhances the effect of the recitation as we are calling Allah directly. Example: Al Aziz, becomes "Ya Aziz celle cellaluhu" (the c in celle cellaluhu will be pronounces as a J – e.g. James)

For the recitation it is recommended to use a so-called "Tasbih" or "Misbaha", a string of prayer beads, usually with 101 or 33 beads (or with various precious stones, a tasbih /Dhikr app will be provided e.g. in IOS or android smartphones). Dhikr, also spelled Zikr, (Arabic: "reminding oneself," or "mention"), is a ritual prayer practiced by Muslims for the purpose of glorifying God and achieving spiritual perfection.This meditation method has a huge impact to our body and our soul. It purifies our heart and frees from negative energies. It has further advantages to our life, which is described in each name.

A recitation is possible anytime and anywhere, even when watching TV or being on a train, in a bus, in a plane, waiting for bus etc. It is highly recommended to perform the Islamic washing before the recitation, but without the washing it's possible as well (e.g. when women have their period, it is not allowed to recite from the Quran, therefore no prayers from the Quran can be recited but the so called Dhikr - also spelled Zikr- the recitation of Allahs 99 Names are allowed at any time without restrictions). Because the recitation of Dhikr protects your body and soul and purifies your heart.

The 99 Names of Allah

(Asma Al Husna)

The recitation of esma al husna brings the body and the soul in a balance. Therefore it is important to recite all Names and not only some of them and see which of the names are especially effective and make us feel well. Every person is different and different names support different characteristics of a person. In general a recitation can take place at anytime and anywhere (the area must be clean) the names of Allah can be recited. They are especially powerful after the morning prayer (Fajr), on Fridays, and after the night prayer (Isha) or before going to bed late at night. According to traditions, Allah will answer any prayer performed at late night hours. To make the recitation even more powerful, the following addition can be added to the name "Celle Celaluhu".

Most commonly used for recitation, this form can also be used to recite the name itself such as El-Malik instead of Ya Malik Celle Celaluhu.

The provided numbers of recitation times are numerological values approved by Islamic scientists and used according to the Arabic alphabeth. It is highly recommended to follow those numbers for any recitation and not use other numbers, because it will affect the purification process and in some cases it could turn the good things into bad (and can make you sick, when using different numbers than the provided ones from the numerological values), for that reason, before following any groups in social media (which is popular currently) please get advice from your local mosque.

The recitation can be continued during a day or a week, it does not need to be completed, once started accordingly. For instance, when reciting the esma "Ya Muzill" 770 times, it is allowed to recite during morning the first half, make a break and recite when you have more time the remaining numbers.

1. Ya Allah –66 times

The only God (apart from whom no God exists). The Highness. The one without comparison. The only adored and worshipped one. The one who unites all His names in this name (also those which we humans do not know yet). Allah ist Nichts gleich und Er besitzt die schönsten Namen (auch die, die wir noch nicht kennen).

This name is the king among the 99 names. Because the name "Allah" contains all 99 Names of Allah known to us humans. Reciting this name balances out our body and soul and brings all the effects that reciting of all 99 names has. It is recommended to recite this name at least 33 times before going to sleep. This name can be recited together with other names or with the words: "Estagfurullah" and "Alhamdulillah"

The name "Allah" occurs 2698 times in the Quran. This Esma supports the answering of prayers and helps to reach a higher status in society and with Allah (spiritually). Especially effective when fasting for 7 days and performing a voluntary prayer (Salah also known as namāz) at night and then reciting this Esma 66 times.

Recitation: "Ya Allah"

The following names can be recited together: „Ya Rahman, Ya Rahim" 298 Mal

2. Ya Rahman – 298 times

The Gracious. The All-merciful. The One who provides everything in the world equally to all (humans, animals and His entire creation). The one who graciously treats everything He has created. The one who makes everything available to everyone in this world. For example, the food from nature, the water and the rain or the sun is equally available to all.

This Name stands for ideal and material wealth and protects against envy. This Name occurs 57 times in the Quran.
Recitation: 298 times "Ya Rahman" at any time or after the obligatory prayers 100 times. Reciting this Esma 100 times for 40 days opens the heart chakra and purifies the heart of all emotional baggage. Also possible:

"Er-Rahmanu'r Rahim" "Ya Rahmanu'r Rahim" 618 times.

3. Ya Rahim–258 times

The (immeasurable and infinite) Merciful One.

For ideal and material prosperity. Protects against or mitigates accidents and problems. Purifies the heart.

This Esma occurs 115 times in the Quran. Reciting after the obligatory prayers 258 times brings protection, prosperity and health. Reciting 100 times daily gains Allah's mercy.

These following Names can be recited together:

Recitation: 258 times "Ya Rahim" or "Ya Rahman, Ya Rahim"

Or "Ya Malik, Ya Quddus (Kuddus) Celle Celaluhu".

4. Ya Malik–90 times

The King. The true Owner of the heavens, the earth and the universe(s). Allah grants kingship (Kingdom, Royalty) to whom He wills and takes kingship from whom He wills.

For ideal and material prosperity. For achieving esteem in the environment. When used regularly and in conjunction with Surah Al-Imran, 26th Ayat (verse) following the recitation, this Esma (quality) increases material prosperity. Pronounce: Maalik

Al-Imran Surah, 26. Ayat (Verse):

„Kuli(A)llâhumme mâlike-lmulki tu/tî-lmulke men teşâu vetenzi'u-lmulke mimmen teşâu vetu'izzu men teşâu vetużillu men teşâ(u)(s) biyedike-lĥ ayr(u)(s) inneke 'alâ kulli şey-in kadîr(un)"

"Thou makest the night to pass into the day, and makest the day to pass into the night. And Thou causest the living to arise out of the dead, and causest death to arise out of the living. You provide for whom You will without measure."

5. Ya Quddûs–170 times

The (only) holy one. (Far from any lack) the perfect one. To whom nothing resembles. To whom the praise is due.

For ideal and material prosperity. For inner peace and well-being.

In the Surah al Jumu´ah (62:1 Quran), 1st Ayat (verse) the following is described:

"All who are in the heavens and on earth glorify (roughly translated:recite, praise) Allah who is Malik, Quddus, Aziz and Hakim".

Recitation: „Ya Quddus" or „Ya Malik, Ya Quddus, Ya Aziz, Ya Hakim"

6. Ya Salâm – 131 times

Salvation. The peace. The one who gives peace. The spotless one.

Salâm means "salvation" in translation. Allah is peace and the bestower of peace. Submitting to Him means finding inner peace. Only those who follow Allah's orders find peace. This Esma (quality) supports perseverance in difficult situations. It supports the answering of prayers, frees from fears, protects from accidents and from evil intentions of other people. It gives healing in physical ailments, gives inner peace and well-being.

In the daily obligatory prayer (namaz), this esma occurs as follows:

„Es-Selamu Aleykum ve Rahmetullah"

Recitation: "Es-Selam, Ya Selam"

7. Ya Mû´min – 136 times

The security. The bestower of security. He who fills the hearts with the light of Allah and with security. He who protects those who confide in Him and cradles them in safety. The one who dispels fears.

"Allah is the only God, besides Allah there is no God. Allah is perfect. Allah is peace, guardian and protector..." (Hasr Surah, 23rd Ayat (verse))

This Esma provides financial security and stability (and independence) and frees from problems. Also, supplications are answered and the heart is purified.

Recitation: "Ya Mumin celle celaluhu"

8. Ya Muhaymin– 145 times

The dominator. The unlimited determiner. The one who watches over everything that He has created. The one who judges everything. The one who keeps everything in control.

Allah sees (watches) everything we do. Even the hidden (our hearts, our thoughts). Only with Allah do we find true protection. This name protects from envy. Helps to know the truth or to know hidden things. The best times to recite it are after the morning prayer (Fajr) and after the afternoon prayer.

The best recitation is as follows: "Ya Muheymin celle celáluhu" (the a is drawn out). Pronounced: Muhaymin

9. Ya Aziz – 94 times

The Almighty. The Honor. The one who cannot be defeated. The one who always wins.

Allah gives power to whom He wills and takes power from whom He wills. Sura Al Burug, verse 16: "Allah does what He wills".

This Esma protects from envy and evil intentions of people, it protects from negative thoughts and energies and it gives inner peace. It can also help the prayers to be answered. Application: 1 hour before evening prayer or at night 94 times or for 40 days 8836 times "Ya Aziz Celle Celaluhu".

10. Ya Jabbaar– 206 times

The subjugator. The one who implements everything at any time. The one who can subdue everything according to His will (at any time). The infinite power.

This Esma should not be recited too often. It emphasizes that Allah is powerful and independent and can implement anything at any time. Allah is constantly in implementation. Furthermore, the Esma (quality) supports the fulfillment of prayers, protects from envy and bad intentions of people. It also frees us from evil people (if they are currently harming us - in this case, we would have to recite 824 times a day). It protects from negative energies and supports the fulfillment of prayers.

Recitation:

"Ya Jabbar" or daily recitation of 1306 times "Ya Jabbar, Ya Zul Celal'i ve'l Ikram celle celaluhu" opens new possibilities in life

11. Ya Mutakabbir– 662 times

The Sublime. The Proud One. The comparatively Greatest and Complete in Himself (means "Perfect"). The one whose work is perfect.

For fame and high status (also prosperity and new opportunities). Helps to be appreciated by society. Also, this Esma protects from negative situations, such as accidents. In direct translation, the word means "arrogance." Allah admonishes us from being arrogant (for our talents or wealth) but recommends us to be down to earth.

Recitation:

"Ya Mutakabbir" or "El-Mutakabbir" or

"Ya Allah, Ya Mutakabbir celle celaluhu" or

"Ya Mutakabbir celle celaluhu"

12. Ya Hâlık – 731 times

The Creator (of heaven and earth and everything in them). The Creator. The One who creates everything from nothing.

Allah determines everything it has created, what these will go through, what will happen to them, down to the smallest detail.

Surah Fatir (Quran), verse 1: "Allah adds to creation what pleases Him".

This Esma stands for the development of new ideas and supports the start of new projects, business start-ups or general success in the profession. It promotes material prosperity.

A recommended recitation is after the morning prayer (Fajr) and a while after the afternoon prayer "Ya Halik" or "El-Halík".

13. Ya Bâri' – 213 timees

The designer. The one who creates everything fitting together. The one who gives a shape to everything. The one who creates everything flawlessly.

This Esma (quality) supports success in new ventures and attaining fame. It supports the answering of prayers and the fulfillment of wishes. Furthermore, it strengthens the memory and frees from negative people in the environment and facilitates to push through difficult projects.

Recitation: „Ya Bari"

213 times or for 7 days 100 times or 45360 times while sitting in the direction of Makkah al-Mukarramah (Ka'bah)

14. Ya Musawwir—336 times

The creator. The creator of the form. The one who gives shape to everything it creates.

This Esma represents beauty and talents (including artistic), aesthetics. Supports to achieve professionalism in difficult tasks or in the profession. Promotes aesthetics, the artistic. It also supports interpersonal relationships and love, as well as to achieve a higher status. It can also be used to highlight or discover one's own beauty.

Recommended recitation time:

"336 times Ya Musavvir" after morning prayer. In the time of the morning prayer

On Thursdays after the afternoon prayer (during this time)

1000 times before falling asleep, after night prayer

"ya Wadud, ya Musawwir, Ya Fettah, Ya Celil," can be recited together

15. Ya Gaffâr – 1281 times

The (always) Forgiving One. The one who covers the sins. The Forgiving one The tirelessly merciful.

Sure Al Fath, verse 14: "He forgives whom He wills and punishes whom He wills"

When recited daily, this esma (name) protects from sins, forgives sins, helps out of grief and gives protection. Furthermore, it frees from negative energies and gives serenity. When reciting regularly it will protect from having accidents and from evil.

Recitation: "Ya Gaffar" after the afternoon prayer, most efficient on Friday´s afternoon or in the midnight.

16. Ya Kahhâr –(should not be recited regularly) 306 times

The Subjugator. The Conqueror. The (All It Has Created) Conqueror.

This esma conquers evil and protects good. It can be recited when feeling oppressed or someone is harming us (to get out of that situation and escape from the tormentor). In the mentioned situations, it will help to reach freedom and safety. Moreover, this esma should not be recited regularly when there is no such situation, because it can harm the reciting person. In the Quran it occurs together with another esma: "Ya Kabiz"

Sure Qasas, 81. Ayat (verse):

„Vekfíní Yâ Kâbíz Yâ Kahhâr, hadita´te mekrihim vardudhum a´nni mezmunine medhurine bi taksir-í tagyir-i tedmir-i. Fe ma kane lehu min fiétin yensurunehu min dun íllah"

translation:

" ...then we caused him to be swallowed up from the earth and also in his house. And he had no multitude to help him against Allah, nor coud he save (himself)..."

The following three caracteristics can be recited together

Recitation: „Ya Wehhab, Ya Razzaq, Ya Fettah" or individually as described below. The number here should be 489 times, more or less as needed. Or 33 times a day after the morning prayer (Fajr) and after the night prayer (Isha).

17. Ya Wehhâb – 14 times

The One Who Supports Without Reciprocation. The bestower of gifts without measure. The One who fills the hearts of His elect with faith. Spoken: Wachaab

This esma means that Allah gives people more than they need to live, regardless of whether they will thank Allah for it or serve Allah. Allah distributes according to His discretion.

For an easy and wealthy life without obstacles, for listening to prayers. For the fast repayment of debts or to get out of debts, recite this esma 196 times.

Recitation: "Ya Wehhab celle celaluhu" or as described above. It is said to be especially effective on Fridays after the morning prayer.

18. Ya Razzaq – 308 times

The Provider. The One who always provides (to His servants anything they need). The One who gives everyone what is needed (materially).

Allah gives food and water in nature to every living creature (thus guaranteeing sustenance to each of His creatures).

This esma stands for success, material prosperity, higher salary, better work. An optimal time to recite is after the night prayer, at midnight or after the Friday prayer (noon prayer).

Recitation: „Ya Razzaq" 308 times and then the following phrase:

„Innelláhe huve-rezzáku zulkuvvetilmetín" oder:

„Ya Mecíd Ya Razzák" 308 Mal oder "El Rezzak, Ya Rezzak"

19. Ya Fettâh – 489 times

The Commanding one. The One Who opens and gives victory. The one who dissolves the obstacles. The One who lightens the heavy. The One who opens the doors (provides possibilities)

This esma is recited for prosperity, for success in certain endeavors, and for interpersonal relationship. It is also recited to promote new encounters.

The best time to recite is after the morning prayer (Fajr) and after the afternoon prayer.

Recitation: as described above or "El Fettah", "Ya Rezzak" or "Ya Fettah (celle celaluhu)"

20. Ya Alîm – 150 times

The Omniscient. The Knowledge. The Science. The infinitely Knowing.

Allah knows everything and knows every detail, every secret about everything He has created. Allah knows the hidden in the hearts and in the minds.

This esma stands for wisdom and knowledge. It supports learning new things or studying. It facilitates all learning and acquiring knowledge. When reciting regularly it supports to learn hidden knowledge, to learn secrets and to widen the knowledge. The best time to recite is after the morning prayer and after the afternoon/ evening prayer.

Recitation: „Ya Alim"

To open the heart chakra, recite after each prayer 100 times following phrase:

"ya Alimel gaybi vesh-shehaadeh (read as written) Or

"ya Aallaamel Guyuub" 100 times after each prayer to gain wisdom and open the heart chakra.

21. Ya Kâbıd – 903 times

The Refuser. The One Who grasps and pulls together.

In Quran this esma is mentioned together with death. It stands for oppressing, suppressing, creating obstacles, as well as forbidding, preventing or withholding. Such as the scarcity of food or wealth. Allah aggravates and brings obstacles as a test (to Whom He Wills). It also represents drought (no rain falls for a long time in some regions). This esma can be recited when trying to lose or lower the weight because it suppresses the appetite. Additionally, it can be recited for changing some behaviors, such as quitting to smoke. This name can be recited to praise Allah or to free oneself from people who harm one and gives negative energy. This name brings us out of danger and provides protection and safety.

Recitation: 903 times "Ya Kabid" for 21 days

For special recitation, when having a certain wish or having a certain problem that needs to be solved, first pray and ask Allah for it, then recite: 70.000 times "Ya Kabid" - to be completed within 21 days. If your wish does not harm other people and is good for you, Allah will answer to it.

22. Ya Bâsıt – 72 times

The spreading One. The Abundant bestower without measure.

This esma stands for positive energy, helps out of mental discomfort, mental disorders, anxiety and provides positive thoughts. Brings more positivity in daily life, to be lucky and happy (luck does not exist in the form, because Allah leaves nothing to chance and defines everything in our lives, without permission of Allah not even a leaf falls from a tree -Sura En´Am) this esma provides more positive moments and happiness and strengthens the memory when reciting regularly.

Recitation: "Ya Basit Allamu´l-guyub celle claluhu" or

"Ya Basit celle celaluhu"

23. Ya Hâfid –1481 times

The humiliator. The One bringing down from above.

It can be understood as a descent in life (when one falls down from the current status and loses the status). Reciting this esma frees us from people who harm us and brings us to safety.

Hafid means „light" or „light-weight" or „gentle". Recitation: on Sundays, or after the morning prayer is recommended

"Ya Hafid celle celaluhu" 1481 times (against evil) or 500 times (so that projects succeed or supplications are heard) it should not be recited too often.

24. Ya Râfi'–351 times

The One Who brings forth. The One Who rises. The Uplifting
One.

This esma stands for rise and is interrelated with the previous
esma "El-Hafid". It helps to get status and power among people,
one rises to a higher position in the profession, gets more wealth
or achieves prosperity. This name is powerful also for health is-
sues. It frees from negative energies and gives inner peace as well
as new positive energy. It purifies your soul and your heart. This
name can also be recited together with "Ya Basit"

Recitation: „Ya Rafi, Ya Basit Celle Celaluhu" or "Ya Rafi celle
celaluhu"

25. Ya Muizz – 117 times

The Glorious One. The One Who gives power. The One Who
gives glory (to whom He wants). The Victorious. The Bestower
of honor.

This esma protects against poverty and helps out of poverty. For
material prosperity. For advancement, protection and safety. Recitation: after the morning prayer (Fajr), at midnight. Can be recited
together with „Mubdi, Wadud. Pronounced: Muis.

26. Ya Muzill – 770 times

The Humiliator. The One Who brings (whom He wants) to defeat. The One Who brings (whom He wants) to descent. The One Who taks away fame and prosperity.

Represents descent, helplessness, despair, humiliation and other problems and needs (for example as a result of greed for wordly things) This esma protects us from the negative caused by people who harm us and frees us from these people and the environment that is not good for us. Pronounced: Muzill

Recitation: 75 times „Ya Muzill" followed by an obligatory prayer (2 sessions called "Rakat") most effective for protection and answering of prayers. Recommended is to recite on Tuesday after the morning prayer.

27. Ya Semi – 180 times

Th All Hearing One. The One Who hears (and answers) the prayers. Allah exist always and is everywhere (at all times).

Allah hears all prayers and hears us when we recite, at all times. This Esma supports the hearing (answering) of prayers. Recite 880 times and read Surah Maryam (19:1 Quran) before falling asleep (turn to your right side to sleep) helps to find out the truth about a question in your mind or helps to make a decision. Recitation: 180 times „Ya Semi Celle Celaluhu" or 540 times „Ya Semi, Ya Basír celle celaluhu" or "Ya Semiu celle celaluhu"

28. Ya Basîr – 302 times

The All Seeing One. The All Hidden Seeing One.

This esma helps to realize the truth and strengthens interpersonal relationships. It also opens the heart chakra, purifies the heart and strengthens the memory. Recitation: (after the morning prayer most effective) „Ya Basir Celle Celaluhu" or „Ya Allahu Ya Basir"

29. Ya Hakim–68 times

The Supreme Judge. The One Who establishes justice. The Wise One.

This esma supports interpersonal relationships, helps to get right, regain rights. Furthermore, it helps to achieve knowledge and purifies the heart and the soul.

Recitation: 68 times, 78 times for more prestige and respect in society. For physical healing recite when you feel ill.

A special recitation for answering of prayers: fast for 3 days and recite 4624 times „Ya Hakim" or „Ya Hakim Celle Celaluhu"

30. Ya Adl–104 times

The Infinetly (Absolutely) Just. The Eternal justice. Pronounced:Adil

Supports getting justice (or what one is entitled to and is denied by others) and strengthens interpersonal relationships. Similar to "Ya Hakim". Strengthens one´s sense of justice and helps one to prosper. This esma establishes justice. For example, in Surah Al-Anam, 115th Ayat (verse), the esma "El Adl" is mentioned.

Recitation: „Ya Adl" or „Ya Adl Celle Celaluhu" 104 times

31. Ya Lâtif – 129 times

The Friendly One. The One Who knows all wishes, all prayers. The One Who knows every detail about everything (that exists /that He has created).

Allah knows all our wishes and if we recite this esma abundantly Allah will make our wishes come true (if these wishes and prayers are good for us and do not harm others, and we are ready to receive them). This name supports the fulfillment of material and ideal wishes and prayers. Recitation: „El-Latif, Ya Latif" 258 times or „Bismillahil-Latif" 9 times or „Ya Latif" 133 times. Particularly powerful is the recitation: El-Latif, Ya Latif' or "Bismillahil-Latif'

Pronounce: Latief

32. Ya Habîr – 812 times

The All Embracing Connoisseur. The Knowledgeable One. The One Who knows the hidden things. The One Who knows all secrets.

This esma strengthens the memory. Supports to be able to grasp things faster and to uderstand better. It can also be recited together with the name „El-Latif" Recitation: „Ya Habir" or „El-Habir Ya Habir" or „Ya Latif Ya Habir" a recitation for 40 days and 7000 repetitions is said to be particularly powerful and answers many prayers.(with Allah´s will).

33. Ya Halim – 88 times

The (Eternally) Patient One. The Good-Natured. The Gentle One. The Forbearing.

This esma emphasizes that Allah takes His time with the reckoning.

In case of stress and aggression or inner turbulences (hyperactivity, anxiety, edginess, nervosity) this esma can be recited, because it brings inner peace and balances out the feelings and provides serenity. It also helps to stand away (quit) from bad habits. It can be recited when giving up hope in something, to gain hope again and to find a solution (with Allah´s will)

Recitation: "Ya Halim celle celaluhu"

34. Ya Azîm–1020 times

The Uniquely Glorious. The Unimaginably Great.

The greatness of Allah does not fit into our imagination. We can only conjecture about the greatness of God. This esma promotes interpersonal communication and relationship. We are better appreciated by thos around us. It helps us achieve a higher status in society and at work.

Recitation: after the morning-/afternoon prayer „Ya Azim "

35. Ya Gafûr–1286 Mal

The Forgiver. The Ever (and Eternally) Forgiving One.

Allah forgives our sins and helps us to have the right values in life. This esma helps us to let go of bad habits and find the right path in life. Furthermore, it cures ailments and dispels fears. It also helps to be able to recite the Shahada (at the deathbed).

Recitation: after the morning- /afternoonprayer „Ya Gafur Celle Celaluhu"

36. Ya Şekûr – 526 times

The Ever Giving One. The One Who gives abundantly. The One to Whom gratitude is due.

This esma gives new energy and helps to realize projects (which one otherwise postpones). It purifies the heart and helps to always have enough of the things you need in life, like food (if you recite before eating) Shekur means to give thanks to Allah. Allah returns to us many times over all the good we do in God´s name for other people or for animals (or when we share our wealth or food with those in need) This name should be recited before reciting other esma´s to express the thank to Allah and this in turn will make your wishes come true and protect you from poverty in life. This name helps to have more positive events in life and for material prosperity. Pronounce: Shekuur

Sure At-Tagabun Verse 17:

„If you give a loan to Allah, He will multiply it for you many times over and forgive you, and Allah is Grateful (Es-Shekur), Forbearing and Compassionate (Al Halim)"

Recitation: "Es Shekur, Ya Shekur" (Esch Schekur) or "Ya Shekur celle celaluhu"

37. Ya Aliyy – 110 times

The Most High. The Exalted. The Mighty One. The true Possessor of power and greatness.

This Esma helps to gain wisdom and expand your knowledge. It protects from humiliation by others and gives prosperity as well as independence.

Recitation: after the morning prayer or after the afternoon prayer: „Ya Aliyy" or: „Aliyyul Aziym"

This name supports that the supplications are heard faster and gives protection.

In Sura An-Nisa, verse 34 it stands:

„...Allah is Exalted and Great" however I would like to correct something that is interpreted wrong in most cases from this sura: "..so beat them..." which refers to women and is not translated correct. Allah and His prophet did never instruct to beat women or kids. Our prophet, the Messenger of Allah, peace be upon him, had never beaten his wife nor had used any form of violence, on the contrary, he instructed all men to always treat their wives well (there are hadith´s on this). Specific words are used in arabic which does not exist in other languages and therefore it is in specific cases translated wrong, because people tried to interpret the meaning based on their knowledge.

38. Ya Kabîr – 232 times

The Greatest of All. The immeasurably Great. The incomparably Great.

Only Allah knows the true greatness of this esma. For material and ideal added value, high status, respect and appreciation in the environment. It also supports interpersonal relationships. It is said that this esma is the key to happiness. Reciting regularly will bring happiness, with Allah´s will.

The Knower of the unseen and the seen, the Most Great, the Most High (Surah Ar-Ra'd , verse 9)

Pronounced: Kebir

Recitation: after the morning prayer (Fajr), just before sunrise or after the afternoon prayer.

Prayer:

„Ya Kebiyru entellezi la tehdil ukulu li vasfi azametih"

is to support getting out of debts.

39. Ya Hafîz – 998 times

The Omniscient One. The Preserver and Sustainer. The One who covers all errors.

To protect the „Nafs", i.e. certain desires for wordly things that are forbidden to us by Allah, things that make us ill or harm us in different ways or hinder us away from turning to Allah

This name also stands for ideal and material prosperity. It protects from problems and envy. In Surah At-Tawba, 11th verse Allah says "I brought up the nafs from the mumin" in some translations this verse is often translated with material things which is not correct. The Nafs is an inherent part of you. It is your inner self. It can direct you towards evil, therefore it is recommended to control your "nafs". There are three types of Nafs: The inciting nafs (an-nafs al-'ammārah), the self-accusing nafs (an-nafs al-luwwāmah), the nafs at peace (an-nafs al-muṭma'innah). It is recommended to read this verse from the Quran often:

„İnnallâheşterâ minel mu'minîne enfusehum ve emvâlehum bi enne lehumul cenneh(cennete), yukâtilûne fî sebîlillâhi fe yaktulûne ve yuktelûne va'den aleyhi hakkan fît tevrâti vel incîli vel kur'ân(kur'âni), ve men evfâ bi ahdihî minallâhi, festebşirû bi bey'ıkumullezî bâya'tum bih (bihî), ve zâlike huvel fevzul azîm(azîmu).„ (At-Tawba, 111. verse)

40. Ya Mukıyt – 550 times

The Protector, the Nurturer. The All Providing One. The Provider.

Allah can create everything and provide it to people (like food in nature) and gives those in need what they need to live. When you are in need and you feel desperate and all of a sudden someone provides you help or something great happens and your problem is solved, all of this happens because Allah helps you when you are in need.

pronounced: Mukiit

This name brings serenity, inner peace and gives (physical) strength, as well as increases material prosperity.

Recitation: „Ya Mukyit Celle Celaluhu"

41. Ya Hasîb – 80 times

The accountable One. The One Who Accounts.

Allah will hold us all accountable for our deeds and will not neglect every little detail. Allah knows all the existing details and calculates all our deeds in this world. This name helps us to be down to earth. Repels people with bad intentions towards us and protects us from danger (also from wild animals when we are in nature). Recitation: 77 times or 99 times „Hasbiyel Hasib" after reciting „El-Hasib" 80 times or „Ya Hasib Celle Celaluhu"

42. Ya Celil – 73 times

The Majestic. The Limitless. The Sublime.

Allah is Great and Has no limits. The power of Allah is limitless.

This esma protects us from negative influence and people with bad intentions towards us. Furthermore, this name gives strength (material and physical) and promotes good habits and interpersonal relationships. Also, this name supports to reach a higher status and more prestige in society. Recitation: „Ya Celil Celle Celaluhu"

43. Ya Kerim – 270 times

The Noble. The Magnanimous. The Generous. The Honorable.

This esma strengthens positive energies and helps to become happier. It gives serenity and inner peace. Especially among women, this esma is popular and is said to have an effect. It is salso said to help to more prosperity (ideal and material). pronounced: Keriim

Recitation: „El-Kerim" or „Ya Kerim"

„Ya Allah, Ya Kerim, Ya Wehhab" helps to be powerful and is effective in hearing supplications.

44. Ya Rakîb–312 times

He Guarding One. The Watchful Observer.

Allah guards and protects everything that Allah has created.

This esma strengthens the memory and gives protection (especially from negative energies). It cleanses and protects one´s aura as well as gives serenity.

Recitation: „Ya Rakib Celle Celaluhu"

45. Ya Mucib – 55 times

The Listener. The One Who hears the prayers.

Allah answers to all prayers, especially when we are in need.. pronounced.: Mudshieb

This esma hears prayers and promotes interpersonal rela

Recitation: „Ya Mucib" or „Ya Mucib, El Mucib" (especially powerful and leads to hearing the prayers). Supports to have a strong relationship. After the recitation of this esma the recitation of Surah aSh-Sharh (Surah 94) .is powerful and strengthens relationships.

46. Ya Vâsi' – 137 times

The All-Encompassing one. The All-Knowing. The Infinitely Merciful.

For a healthy and content life as well as for an inner balance.

In some interpretations, this esma is described as supporting to have a „long life", which is not translated correct. Allah has predermined the time, how long we will live, before we were born and the age we will reach to the minute. We cannot push the time forward or backward one minute. We can only pray and recite to live as contentedly and healthily as possible.

Recitation: "Ya Vasi celle celaluhu"

47. Ya Hakîm – 78 times

The Wise. The Commanding One. The Judge. The Perfectly Powerful one. The perfect Power.

This esma supports to be appreciated by the society, supports gaining knowledge and motivates improve yourself, to learn and to study.

Pronounced: Hakiim (means Judge)

Recitation: "Ya Hakim celle celaluhu"

48. Ya Wadûd – 20 times

The Loving One. The One Who Lovingly turns to others. The One Who embraces everything with Love.

Recommended is the recitation after the night prayer (Isha) especially powerful and in combination with following names "Ya Camii" , "Ya Mucib", "Ya Mubdi" "Ya Muizz" and Surah „Al-Fatiha"

It supports love and interpersonal relationships. Supports to find someone, to marry or to have new friends. When we were born, Allah has put in our hearts the meaning and power of this esma. Any human being has "Wadud" in their hearts. This is why this esma has a strong effect when reciting for improving relationships. The recitation is most effective on monday.

Recitation:

1st option: 21 times Al-Fatiha, followed by 21 times Ya Wadûd

2nd option: 7 times Al-Fatiha followed by 33 times "Ya Wadûd ,Ya Cami"

3rd option: "Ya Wadud, Ya Mubdi, Ya Muid, Ya Muizz, Ya Mucib"

4th option: "Ya Wadud" 20 or 1001 times on Mondays

A subsequent recitation of Surah Ad-Duha (Surah 93) is said to be particularly powerful and strengthens relationships

49. Ya Macîd – 57 times

The Glorious One. The All Forgiving.

With this name Allah helps us achieve fame and status in society. It helps to gain material prosperity and more prestige in the society. When reciting regularly, this esma can increase knowledge.

Recitation: „Ya Macid Celle Celaluhu" daily 48 times 57 times or 100 times

50. Ya Bâis–573 times

The Raiser of Death. The One Who Sent the prophets into the Earth.

Allah has the power to raise all the death. When Allah says "become" whatever Allah wills, will become immediately.

This esma helps to create more wealth (more profit, higher salary). It provides to feel the fear of God in the heart and keep human being away from people with bad intentions.

Recitation: „ Ya Bais, Ya Fettah Celle celaluhu" or "Ya Bais Celle Celaluhu"

51. Ya Şehîd – 319 times

The One Who is always present. The Witness of everything that happens (in the universes He has created)

„...Allah is sufficient as a witness..." (surah En-Nisa, verse 79)

„...Allah is Witness over everything..." (surah Al Hajj, verse 17)

This name supports interpersonal relationships, it gives calmness and serenity. Pronounced: Shehiid

Recitation: „Ya Sehid Celle Celaluhu"

52. Ya Hakk – 108 times

The Truthful. The Absolute Truth. The One Whose existence does not change. The One Who Exists Steadfastly.

This name strengthens the faith. It helps to finish what has been started and reveals what is hidden. It improves the current situation and supports being appreciated in the society. It also cures diseases and helps to pray and recite in the right way.

Recitation: „Ya Hakk Celle Celaluhu"

53. Ya Wekil – 66. times

The Trusted One. The Deputy. The Expert.

The One Who finishes what is left to Allah. The One Who Sets everything right and Finishes it.

When we leave certain things to Allah, it will be done and completed or solved with Allah´s will. Things that we cannot influence in life like destiny. Wekil means to act on behalf of. If we leave things to Allah in our prayers or through this recitation that we are not able to solve, Allah will solve it for us (with Allahs will). Pronounced: Vekil

Recitation: „Ya Wekil Celle Celaluhu"

Surah Al-Muzzammil, verse 9:

„(Allah is) the Lord of the East and the West. There is no God but Allah. So take Allah as your vicegerent (Wekil)."

Recite following phrase after reciting „Ya Wekil":

„Rabbu-lmeşriki velmaġribi lâ ilâhe illâ huve fetteḣ iżhu vekîlâ(n)"

54. Ya Kawiyy–117 times

The Strong. The Powerful. The Powerful One. The Power.

Aslo: The One Who provides His faithful servants (Mumin) with everything (what Allah wants) in the hereafter.

Allah´s power is infinite and beyond our imagination. Allah´s power knows no bounds and has no boundaries. Allah influences everything and everyone, but nothing can influence Allah. This name gives strength (also physical), protects from accidents and negative events. It also cures diseases.

Recitation: „El Kawiyy, Ya Kawiyy"

55. Ya Metîn – 500 times

The (in every respect) Strong One. The (reliably) steadfast.

For ideal and material prosperity and longevity of this prosperity. For steadfastness in faith. Protects from diseases and gives strength. (physical). It promotes good habits and frees from bad habits. Frees us from people, who harm us or are not good for us.

Recitation: "Ya Metin Celle Celaluhu" or "El-Kawiyyul Metin" 10 times or Ya Kawiyy, Ya Metin Celle Celaluhu"

Surah Al-Baqara (Bakara), 153th Verse:

„...seek help in steadfastness and prayer! Allah is with the steadfast."

56. Ya Weliyy – 46 times

The Patron (of anyone who needs His protection and guidance)
The True friend and Helper of the believers (the Mu`min).

With this name we can ask for help. Also for spiritual assistance
and for inner peace as well as inner strength.

This esma supports the attainment of a higher status (with Allah
and in society). With Allah, everyone is equal. There are only different levels in faith. Human being can reach a higher level in faith
and be closer to Allah by reciting and praying. For inner restlessness, recite this esma 46 times daily.

Recitation: „Ya Weliyy" , „El Weliyy", „Ya Weliyyu Ya Allah"or
„Ya Weliyy Celle Celaluhu"

„Allah is the Protector of the Faithful"

(Muhammad surah, Verse 11)

57. Ya Hamîd – 68 times

The Praiseworthy. The One Worthy of Praise. The One to praise. The One to thank.

With this name, we thank Allah and praise Allah´s power and various facets. The more we thank and praise Allah, the more we will be rewarded. Pronounced: Hamied

Recitation: after the morning prayer „Ya Hamid Celle Celaluhu" or 99 times when asking Allah for help.This esma is recited for popularity in society, for good a good character and for success in profession.

Surah Fatir, verse 15:

„... you are poor and depend on Allah, but Allah depends on nothing and no one and is worthy of praise"

58. Ya Muhsî – 148 Mal

The One Who records everything. The One Who knows all numbers. The One Who knows about every single detail (in the universes Allah has created and in the hearts of a human being)

This name strengthens the memory and perceptiveness. Supports interpersonal relationships.

Recitation: Friday midnight, 100 times or 1000 times, on other days 148 times.

„La ilahe illalau´l Muhsi" is said to be particularly effective. „Ya Muhsi Celle Celaluhu" is possible as well.

59. Ya Mubdi' –56 times

The Originator of all creation. The All-Creating One from the beginning. The All Unique Creator. The One Who creates everything from nothing.

This esma helps us out of situations where we no longer had hope or we receive help, which we no longer expected. It helps to succeed and reveals hidden things. It facilitates the making of decisions when recited 1000 times. It also strengthens the memory. In case of pregnancy, reciting „Ya Mubdi" 99 times is said to protect the baby. Pronounced: Muubdi

In Connection with the recitation of the names "Wadud, Muid, Muizz, Muid" it is intented to strengthen love and interpersonal relationships, as well as to promote new encounters.

Recitation:

„El-Mubdi, Ya Mubdi" or

„El-Mubdi" or "Ya Mubdi" or

„Ya Wadud, Ya Mubdi, Ya Muid, Ya Muiz" or

„El-Mubdi, Ya Mubdi"

60. Ya Muid – 124 times

The All-Creating, All-Destroying, and All-Re-Creating (creating after destroying). The One Who revives (brethes life into) everything. The One Who brings (every creation) back to life.

This esma supports recovering missed opportunities or making the best use of current opportunities. In connection with the recitation of the names „Wadud, Muizz, Mubdi" it is said to trengthen love and interpersonal relationships and to be calm, sensitive and lovely in friendships and relationships. It also relieves psychological problems and gives inner peace and contentment.

Recitation: „Ya Muid" or

„Ya Muid Celle Celaluhu" or

„Ya Mubdi, Ya Muid Celle Celaluhu" 181 times

For achieving goals and answering of prayers. It also strengthens the memory.

61. Ya Muhyî – 68 times

The Giver of Life. The Health Giver. The Merciful.

This esma supports success in the profession. It does also support to regain health or to keep the health. Also, it cleanses the heart and gives inner peace.

Surah Ghafir, Verse 68 (the Forgiver):

"Allah calls to life and lets die"

Recitation:

„Ya Muhyi" or

„Ya Muhyi Celle Celaluhu" or

"El Muyi, Ya Muhyi" 68 times for success, 1001 cleanses the heart, 4624 times for healing diseases.

62. Ya Mumît –i.d.R. not recite

The One Who determines the dying. The One Who creates death.

Allah has provided a certain time for every living being to live. This.

Recitation: after the morning prayer 295 times 409 times, 490 times „Ya Mumit Celle Celaluhu" frees from negative influences, negative habits and everything negative that is condemned by other people in our lives. Allah guides those who recite this esma other people in our lives. Allah guides those who recite this esma 490 times, turning completely to Allah.

63. Ya Hayy – 18 times

The Living One. The Eternally Living One. The Owner over the life. The One Who lives from himself (independently).

Allah is alive at all times. This quality represents health and good well-being. It heals pyhsical ailments and gives new energy. It strengthens interpersonal relationships and appreciation in society. Recitation: 324 times (18x18) „Ya Hayy Celle Celaluhu" times to praise Allah, 18 times to praise Allah.

„Ya Hayyu Ya Kayyum" or „Ya Allah Ya Hayyu Ya Kayyum" 184 times for answering prayers and for protections from negative events.

64. Ya Kayyûm–156 times

The One Who Exists in Himself. The One Who holds the heavens (there are several) and the earth and everything that is in between. The One Without whose help nothing can exist. The One Who exists independently (is not dependent on any help). The One Who keeps (all living beings) alive. Pronounced: Kayyuum

Recitation: 16 times, 40 times or

156 times, 174 times, 870 times „Ya Hayyu Ya Kayyum" or

„Ya Hayyu Ya Kayyum la ilahe illa ente"

This esma purifies the heart and mind answers prayers, frees from negative or difficult situations (solves problems) and strengthens the memory.

Baqara surah, verse 255: „There is no God but Allah, He is Hayy and Kayyum (always alive and independently existing)"

65. Ya Vâcid – 14 times

The One Who brings being. The Shaper. The One Who gives form to all things. The independent One. The One whose wealth never decreases (and always remains the same).

This esma is to help find lost things and preserve the property. Also it supports health.

In the Qur´an, the esma: „Vacid" occurs in the following surah:

Ad-Duha sura, 7. Ayat (Verse): „Ve vecedeke dâllen fe hedâ."

Translation: „He has found you and guided you (on the right path)"

66. Ya Mâcid – 48 times

The Glorious. The Rich. The (infinetly) Generous.

This esma strenthens our faith, gives us inner peace, praises Allah´s wealth and asks for material or ideal support.

Recitation: 100 times (daily) „Ya Macid Celle Celaluhu" after the obligatory prayers brings prosperity and esteem in the society. Reciting 48 times daily helps to achieve a higher level and status.

67. Ya Vâhid – 19 times

The One and Only. Allah is Unique.

There is nothing that resembles Allah. In surah Al-Ikhlas (pronounced: Al Ihlas) Allah is described. The surah begins with "Kul huvallahu Ehad… – which means Allah is Unique! This surah was among those to receive many different titles. It is a short declaration of tawhid. This esma purifies our heart, helps to cast off ballast and supports the fulfillment of desires in connection with regular prayer. It also strengthens us in our faith.

Recitation: "Ya Vahid" 19 times

68. Ya Samed–134 times

The Eternal. The independent.

Allah is the Only we surrender to, our Only hiding place. Our Only place to go. This esma brings independence and protects from negative energies of people around us. Furthermore, this esma can be recited to gain knowledge of hidden things and get answers of questions.

Recitation: 134 times „Ya Samed Celle Celaluhu" in connection with surah Al Ikhlas for the answering of prayers

Also possible: 100 times „Ya Ferd Ya Samed Celle Celaluhu" for gaining Allahs goodwill. Reciting in combination with Surah Maryam (Arabic synonym of "Mary"): read surah Maryam once, then recite the esma "ya Samed" before laying down to sleep.

Insa Allah you will find the answer of your question…

69. Ya Qâdir – 305 times

The One Who enforces His destiny. The Onw Who has the true power to do (and create) everything.

Allah is the Owner of all power and authority. This esma gives the power to do anything (professionally) that you want to do. For material prosperity and listening of prayers. Furthermore, it protects from negative energies. Pronounced: Kadiir

Recitation: „Ya Qadir Celle Celaluhu" or „Ya Qadir"

Reciting „Ya Kadir, Ya Allah, Ya Rahman, Ya Allah, Ya Rahim Ya Allah, Ya Kerim Ya Allah" 100 times during the night supports the hearing of prayers.

Why recitation is often done at night is because Allah hears the prayers addressed to Him ad night (because one lies awake and forgoes sleep)

70. Ya Muktedir – 744 times

The absolutely Capable.

This Esma praises Allah´s power and helps to succeed. One is also guided rightly by Allah.

Recitation: after the obligatory prayers 744 times „Ya Muktedir Celle Celaluhu" or after the morning prayer 100 times

71. Ya Muqaddim – 184 times

The One Who emphasizes. The One Who pushes everything forward at will and puts everything forward.

This esma represents a higher status in life. It strengthens interpersonal relationships. It helps in studying for exams as well as during the exam, when reciting before taking the exam.

(with Allah´s Will). Pronounced.: Mukaddim.

Recitation: „Ya Mukaddim Celle Celaluhu" or „El Mukaddim"

72. Ya Muahhir – 846 times

The One Who postpones everything and puts it back. The All Slowing Down. The One Who stops.

This esma protects us from negative energies and protects us from people with bad intentions. It helps to achieve forgiveness and purifies the heart. Pronounced: Mu'achir

Recitation: „Ya Muahhir Celle Celaluhu"

Following esma can be recited together in practice:

Recitation: „Ya Awwal, Ya Ahir Celle Celaluhu"

73. Ya Awwal – 37 times

The First. The Beginning.

Allah´s existence has no beginning and no end!

This esma stranslated means "first" and indicates that Allah defines the beginning over everything that Allah has created. This name supports success and also winning in competition. Pronounced: Ewwel

Recitation: „Ya Awwal Celle Celaluhu" 37 times, 1000 times or „Ya Awwal, Ya Ahir Celle Celaluhu"

74. Ya Âhir – 801 times

The Last (however that itself no end possesses)

Allah´s existence has no end! This esma means that Allah defines the End. Allah´s existence is beyond our imagination. Allah exists infinitely. Allah is „Awwal" (before) and „Ahir" (after) everything that He has created. This esma supports positive energies and brings quality in life. Furthermore, the name protects from negative energies and frees from problems. It also purifies the heart. Pronounced: Aahiir

Recitation: „Ya Ahir Celle Celaluhu" or „Ya Awwal Ya Ahir Celle Celaluhu"

75. Ya Zâhir – 1106 times

The Revealed. The visibility. Allah´s existence is visible.

Allah´s existence is provable and everything He created (is informed about it. E.g. the nature, the people, the animals, the food, the water, the mountains, the seas. Everything proves Allah´s existence and is visible to us. (pls note that Allah has no gender, Allah is beyond our imagination, the word He is only a title!) pronounced: Zaahir

This esma helps when you want to know the truth about certain things, it reveals hidden things, helps against aggression and gives inner peace.

Hadid surah, verse 3: Allah is Ahir, Zahir, Awwal and Batin"

recitation: „Ya Zahir Celle Celaluhu" or „Ez Zahir" or „Ya Zahir"

76. Ya Bâtın – 62 times

The Hidden. The Secret.

Allah is not visible to all that He has created. Allah has no form and no gender. It is forbidden to imagine Allah as a form. Allah is beyond our imagination. We are only a part of what Allah has created. Allah is limitless and infinite and does not fit into any particular frame or shape. Pronounced: Baatín

Recitation: after the morning prayer or after the afternoon prayer is the best time, but it is possible to recite any time 62 times or 3844 times (62x62) „ Ya Batin, Ya Zahir" or „El Batin, Ya Batin" or „Ya Batin"

This esma protects from negative energies opens the heart chakra, gives inner peace and balances out the emotions, cleanses the heart from emotional ballast and dispels fears, and anxiety. By reciting it many times, one is guided by Allah and prayers are answered.

77. Ya Wâli – 47 times

The Protector. The One Who governs everything (alone). The patron.

Allah watches over the heavens (several!), the earth and the universes. Allah rules alone. In support of this, there is the surah Al-Ikhlas where Allah is described. This esma purifies the heart and frees us from ballast. For inner balance. Pronounced: Waalii

recitation: "Ya Wali"

78. Ya Mutaâli – 551 times

The Pure and High Possessor of all great qualities (and virtues). Allah´s majesty and purity is beyond human description. Beyond our imagination.

This esma supports the achievement of certain goals in life by lightening the heavy. The name protects us from mistakes as well as from accidents and problems. It brings inner balance and serenity. It protects from people with bad intentions and helps to listen to prayers.

Recitation: „Ya Mutaali Celle Celaluhu" or „Ya Mutaali"

79. Ya Barr – 202 times

The righterous. The Charitable. The Helper. The One Who enlightens His servants.

This esma indictes the wealth and generosity of Allah. Allah is richer than we can imagine and very generous. Allah rewards whom He wills with how much He wills. All our success and wealth are obtained by Allah´s permission and by Allah himself. It is not right to think that we have achieved something by our own efforts, because Allah is with us all the time and supports us, when He wills. Allah rewards whom He wills. Here is also hidden the name that Allah forgives and covers our mistakes and sins (e.g. so that others do not know them). This esma supports that good things happen to us. Pronounced: Berr. Recitation: also possible: „Ya Berr"

80. Ya Tawwâb – 409 times

The One Who accepts the repentance of His servants. The One Who receives and mitigates repentance.

Allah forgives our faults and accepts any repentance we have when we turn to Allah with all our faults and sins and ask for forgiveness. Provided we have true repentance in our hearts, Allah will forgive us. In practice. One should additionally perform two rakat "Tawbah" prayer (repentance prayer) as a sign that we regret our mistakes and do not want to repeat them, that we turn away from our mistakes. With Allah´s will, we will not repeat them again. Pronounced: Tawwab. There are legends that Allah urges us to constantly seek forgiveness from Allah for our mistakes, even continuously. Recitation: "Ya Tawwab celle celaluhu"

81. Ya Muntaqim –630 times

The righteous avenger. The Avenger. The One Who executes justice. The One Who restores the balance.

Allah always establishes justice.

Some people recite this esma to free themselves from severe situations caused by other people (100 times, 630 times). For instance, when one is constantly attacked (or insulted, bullied, humiliated), when one is oppressed, or when someone makes one´s life difficult in some other way (e.g. uses violence, psychologically or physically). Pronounced: Muntekiim

This esma frees us from the bad (evil) in our lives caused by other people and gives us protection (from people who harm us or treat us badly) these people will then desist and leave us alone. We have someone watching over us and protecting us. All we need to do is to ask for it.

82. Ya Afuvv – 156 times

The Forgiver of sins. The Forgiver.

Allah forgives us whenever we ask Allah for it. This esma is recited very often in practice to gain forgiveness and for answering prayers in combination with other names in this book. It also supports to have more positive events in life (also it opens doors for new opportunities) Pronounced: Afuw

Recitation: "Ya Afuw celle celaluhu"

83. Ya Raûf – 286 times

The Gracious One. The Compassionate One.

Allah´s mercy is beyond our imagination. Whenever we ask for Allah´s mercy, we will receive it.

Reciting this esma purifies the heart, calms the souls, and protects from envy. It also supports interpersonal relationships and promotes communication (usefull in disputes that you want to get out of the way)

Recitation: 287 times „Ya Rauf" creates harmony among friends, family and in marriage.

84. Ya Mâliku'l-Muulk – 212 times

The Owner of All Riches. Eternal Owner of all wealth. The Eternally Wealthy.

Allah is the sole owner of all wealth on earth and in the universe (as well as in the universes). This esma praises Allah´s wealth and prosperity. This name gives prosperity, protects the existing wealth, gives success and independence. For material and ideal prosperity. Also, this name frees from anxiety and protects from poverty. Recitation: "Ya Maliku´l Mulk Ya Zu´l Celali ve´l-Ikram celle celaluhu"

85. Ya Zuu'l-Celâli ve'l-İkrâm. 1098 times

The Majesty. The Honor. The Owner of the Time. The One Who is Worshipped. The Magnificent One. The Highness. The Generous One.

This esma describes several names of Allah at once and stands for prosperity and wealth. Allah possesses the greatness and time, even that which is beyond our imagination. By greatness here is meant and ideal greatness. It also includes wisdom. Allah raises whoever he wants to a higher level. (mentally) in terms of ideal values and that person devotes himself entirely to Allah. Allah lowers whom He wills to a lower level and that person devotes himself entirely to worldly things. This name helps to increase satisfaction, increase prosperity and to overcome obstacles in the profession. Allah lightens the heavy. Pronounced: Sul.Lalali-wal-Ikram

86. Ya Muksit – 209 times

The impartial Judge. The Just One. The One who creates everything without gaps and fitting together in a perfect way.

Allah is perfect and everything He does fits together and is
brought to completion without any gaps. This esma supports
one´s sense of justice, frees from fears and envy, and from aggression. It also gives calmness and serenity.

Recitation: "Ya Muksit celle celaluhu"

87. Ya Câmi' – 114. times

The Gatherer. The One Who Gathers (all).

Allah brings together what belongs together (also humans) and
what is opposed. Allah will bring us together in judgement day to
judge us.

This esma brings together those who are offended by each other
helps with separations and for more popularity in the environment. It can be recited together with the esma: "Ya Wadud" for
better interpersonal relationships and for protections agains sepa-
ration. Pronounced: Dshamii

Recitation: "Ya Cami Celle Celaluhu" or "Ya Wadud Ya Cami"

After reciting this esma the recitation of Al-A´la surah (Surah 87)
is said to be especially powerful and strengthen relationships.

Following names can be recited together:

"Ya Ganiyy Ya Mugni"

88. Ya Ğaniyy–1060 times

The Richest (among the rich). The One Who is enough (for himself) The Abundance.

Allah´s wealth is beyond our imagination. According to legend Allah asked a man "Do you want to possess the whole world and obtain wealth, which only a few had before you? Or do you want to receive my mercy?" and the man said: " My Lord, I do not want the whole world, life is fleeting. Instead, I want Your mercy, which is infinite!" For Allah to make us all the richest in the world is a small matter, for Allah Himself is the Richest of the rich. Pronounced: Ghanii

This esma stand for wealth. Ganiyy means "more than enough" in the sens of "abundance"

89. Ya Muğnî – 1100 times

The Liberator. The Releaser. The Wealth Bestowing.

Wealth is a test by Allah to pass. Allah always tests and rewards us (whether we have gained Allah´s favor or not). If something bad happens to us, it is another test, just like wealth or popularity. The most dangerous test is the one that does not reveal itself as a test, like wealth or popularity. This esma supports material prosperity and frees from fears.

Recitation: "Ya Mugni Celle Celaluhu" oder "Ya Ganiyy Ya Mugni"

90. Ya Mâni' – 161 times

The Restrainer. The Protector. The Preventer. The One Who Restrains the Good and the Bad.

This esma protects against accidents or unexpected problems and controls the "nafs" the (nefs –defined as that which calls us to fulfill our whims and desires and is recognizable in almost every human problem). The name supports answering the prayers, gives security and satisfaction. Pronounced: Manii

Recitation: "Ya Mani Celle Celaluhu"

91. Ya Dârr – 1001 times

The Producer of distress. The Oppressor. The Creator of All Negative events. The Damaging One.

This esma loosely translated means „crushing". Some people recite this esma 1001 times on Fridays, at night, to free themselves from the difficult situations they are currently in. This is said to make one especially close to Allah and protected. Reciting regularly balances out and frees from negative engergies and thoughts.

Recitation: „Ya Dârr celle celâluuhû" 1001 times (101 times possible as well)

92. Ya Nâfi' – 201 times

The Benefactor. The Creator of all that is good. The Promoter of the useful.

Allah creates the healing and all the good in our lives. Allah creates the solution to our problems and the positive. Everything good can only happen if Allah created it. Pronounced: Naafii

This esma has a healing effect. Furthermore, it helps to cope with problems and supports to be successful.

Recitation: „Ya Nâfi celle celâluuhû" is said to protect agains various diseases and problems as well as stress (and everything caused by stress)

93. Ya Nûr – 256 times

The Light. The Owner Who enlightens His servants. The One Who enlightens the hearts. The One Who illuminates the way.

surah 24 (Surah An-Nûr) is also known as the "verse of light". It says "Allah is the light of the heavens and the earth. It goes on to say, "Allah guides to His light whom He wills."

This esma purifies the heart. Helps to see the truth and distinguish it from untruth. Moreover, it protects families. iN connection with the surah Nûr, 35th ayat (verse), this esma is also sait to strengthen the memory.

Recitation: „Ya Nûr" 256 times and the n the surah Nûr 35th Ayat (verse):

Allâhu nûrus semâvâti vel ard(ardı), meselu nûrihî ke mişkâtin fîhâ mısbâh(mısbâhun), el mısbâhu fî zucâceh(zucâcetin), ez zucâcetu ke ennehâ kevkebun durrîyyun, yûkadu min şeceratin mubâraketin zeytûnetin lâ şarkîyetin ve lâ garbiyyetin, yekâdu zeytuhâ yudîu ve lev lem temseshu nâr(nârun), nûrun alâ nûr(nûrin), yehdîllâhu li nûrihî men yeşâu, ve yadribullâhul emsâle lin nâs(nâsi), vallâhu bi kulli şey'in alîm(alîmun).

Verses 36 and 37 can also be recited afterwards, this is said to be particularly powerful so that prayers will be answered.

Translation of surah Nûr, verse 35:

„Allah is the light of the heavens and the earth. Allah´s light is like a niche in which there is a lamp. The lamp is in a glass, the glass is like a twinkling star. Lit (is the lamp) by a blessed olive tree, neither eastern nor western, whose oil would almost shine even if the fire did not touch it. Light upon light. Allah guides to His light whom He wills. And Allah coins parables from men, and Allah knows all things."

94. Ya Hâdi – 20 times

The Guide. The One Who leads to the right way.

This esma supports finding the right path and making the right decisions. Without Allah´s guidance, we would be lost. If needed, this esma can be recited more frequently.

Regular recitation of 400 repetitions helps to achieve success.

Recitation: "Ya Hadi celle celaluhu"

95. Ya Bedi' – 86 times

The unexampled Creator. The Inventor. The Incomparable. The amazing Creator.

Allah's power is amazing and is not comparable to anything that already exists. Allah has created everything, even that which we do not yet know (which is hidden until now). This Esma supports art, aesthetics and provides Allah's support for various concerns.

recitation: "Ya Bedi Celle Celaluhu"

A longer recitation of 70,000 repetitions of "Ya Bedi Celle Celaluhu" provides special protection and support from Allah. 70 repetitions of "Ya Bedias'semavati vel'ardi ya zelcel'ali vel'ikram" provides relief from difficult situations.

Special recitation:

After a general prayer with your desires, recite for 21 days in total 10.000 times "Ya Bedi" and your desire will be fulfilled.

96. Ya Bâki – 113 times

The Eternal Perpetual. The Infinite. The Eternal Creator.

Everything we do in Allah´s name and for Allahs´mercy in this world will be saved for eternity by Allah and we will receive reward for it. This esma supports a healty life, frees from negative energies and gives protection and inner balance. Recitation: after the morning prayer or after the afternoon prayer.

Recitation: after the five obligatory prayers (Namaz)

„Ya Baki Celle Celaluhu"

or after the morning prayer (Fajr) „Ya Baki"

97. Ya Vâris – 707 times

The Only Heir. The (true) Owner of all riches. The Owner of everything visible and invisible.

All the wealth in the world and in the universes that people possess in truth, belongs to Allah. By Allah´s permission, people possess the riches. This esma supports a contented life, frees from discomfort and gives financial security.

Recitation: after the morning prayer (Fajr)

98. Ya Raşîd – 514 times

The Bestower of Righteousness. The One Who leads to the right way. The One Who brings everything t an end (in the right way).

Also: "The Admonisher. The One Who does everything in the right way". This esma supports to be a better person and to do right. It helps agains helplessness and supports to make a decision. (Er- Raşîd)

Recitation: reciting " Ya Reşîd (or: Ya Raşîd) celle celâluuhû " 514 times on a regular basis will assist in discarding or reducing one´s negative qualities in character. It also helps listening to the supplications.

Reciting this esma 1000 times in the evening after the evening prayer (Maghrib) and after the night prayer (Isha) will help one to be alert and careful in professional or other matters.

99. Ya Sabûr – 298 times

The Infinitely Patient. The One Who is Steadfast (in patience).

Sabûr means "patience". Our Prophet Eyyub was especially tested in his patience. (In Surah Sad, 41st- 44th ayat it is briefly explained). He lost his children, all his wealth, and was riddled with illnesses (visible and invisible) for several years. He never stopped reciting Allah´s names all the time and praying to Allah. He kept saying "Allah is enough for me". Until one day he regained everything he has lost and his illnesses were all cured by Allah´s will.

Reciting: 298 times helps to finish what has been started and not yet completed. Furthermore, it teaches us patience for reciting and praying when we are impatient.

Here we learn that if we want to be true believers, we must learn to say "Allah is enough for me" in every situation, whatever happens to us, always expressing our gratitude and understanding that we are in a trial. Our wealth, our health, our family and friends, these are all gifts that Allah has given us.

some examples of combined recitation for well being:

For strength and inspiration

Following names can be recited 100 times for strength and inspiration

Ya Allah

Ya Rahman

Ya Rahim

Ya Hayyu

Ya Kayyum

Ya Kerim

Ya Zul Celal´í ve´l Ikram

Then the surah Fatiha is recited 1 time.

With Allah´s will you´ll find inspiration and strength.

For prosperity and financial security as well as new professional ventures

Ya Malikul Mulk

Ya Zul Celalí Ve´l-Ikram

Ya Ganiyy

Ya Batin

Ya Halik

Ya Wadud 270 times (frees from debts)

For health

Ya Hayy

Ya Hayyu Ya Kayyum

Ya Safi (pronounced: Shaafi)

Abundance

Following prayer is said to be powerful to bring abundance in your life. The prayer calls all four angels and the seven sleepers.
In Christian tradition, the story of the "Seven Sleepers" is the story of a group of youths who hid inside a cave outside the city of Ephesus around 250 AD to escape one of the Roman persecutions of Christians and emerged some 300 years later. The story also appears in the Qur'an (18:9–26).

Recitation: every morning during the morning prayer (fajr) 3 times.

"Ant prayer" (the prayer of an ant)

"Allahuumme ya Rabbi Cebrâîle ve Mîkâile ve İsrâfile ve Azrâile ve İbrahime ve İsmaile ve İshaka ve Yakube ve muunzilel berakâti vet Tevrâti vez-Zebûri vel İncili vel Furkan.
Ve lâ havle ve lâ kuvvete illa billahil aliyyil azim.
Lâ ilâhe illallahuul melikuul hakkul muubin.
Muhammeduu-Resuuluullahi sadikul va'dil emin.
Ya Rabbi, Ya Rabbi, Ya Hayyu, Ya Kayyum, Ya zel Celali vel İkram.
Es'eluuke ya Rabbel arşil azimi en yerzuukani rizkan halalen tayyiben birahmetike ya erhamer Rahimin.
Yemliha, Mekseline, Mislina, Mernuuş, Debernuuş, Şazenuuş, Kefetatayyuş, Kıtmîr.

Recite for 7 days every night 1040 times "Ya Hayyu hiine laa hayye fii deymuumiyyeti mulkihi ve bekiaah Ya Hayy" then recite "Allahu huve melik'un, Semi'un, Qadir'un, Kerim, Halim'un, Latief'un, Alim'un, Muin'un, Sadiiq (Saadiik)

If you feel that everything goes wrong and you have bad luck, you feel you are not in balance, have negative thoughts, then recite the esma

"Ya Rafii" in its defined number (351). Recitation of 351 times every day will bring you in a balance, solves problems, makes happen, what was postponed or rejected so far, helps to complete work and helps to have "luck" and fortune. Try for 21 days.

Recitation Examples in Practice

For the regulation of appetite and to bring the body back into balance

"Subhane Rabbiyel aliyyil a-lel vehhab"

Ya Rahman, Ya Nafi, Ya Malik, Ya Selam, Ya Azim, Ya Mucib

Ya Wadud, Ya Muqtedir, Ya Batin, Ya Nur (in their respective numbers)

And then: surah Yunus, 57th verse 7 times

and then recite Surah Ya-Sin (Yaseen) 1 time

For strengthening love and interpersonal relationships

For answering of prayers

El Wadud, Ya Wadud 400 times or daily 71 times for 7 days

Ya Mubdi

Ya Muid

Ya Mugis

Ya Musawwir

Ya Latif or: Bismillahil-Latif is especially powerful for answering of prayers

or

Ya Wadud and then the surah Ad-Duha (surah 93)

Ya Cami and then surah Al-A'la (surah 87)

Ya Mucib and then surah Ash-Sharh (surah 94)

Or

100 Salawat, 99 Bismillahirrahmanirrahim, 66 Ya Allah,

526 Ya Shekur, 86 Ya Bedi, 1000 Ya Hayy

Salawat

All muslims have been advised to send salam and Darood On Prophet(pbuh) -this is Evident in the Verse 56 of Surah Al Ahzab

There are different version on saying selam to the prophet:

When reciting Allah´s names and after prayers, it is recommended to say this salavat:

Allahumme salli ala seyyidine Muhammedun ne bi ummihi, ve ala alihi ve sahbihi ve selim

Allahuumme salli alâ Seyyidinâ Muhammedin ve alâ âlihî ve sahbihî ve bârik ve sellim

Short salavat besides the prayers and the recitation:

as-salamu 'alaika ayyuhannabiyyu wa rahmatullahi wa barakat-u-hu.

as-salamu alaika ya Rasul-Allah or.

As Salamu laikum ya Khateman-nabiy.

For answering of a certain prayer...

(when having a certain wish or problem)

Firstly, do the prayer and ask Allah for help (for making it true, for making it solved, for support)

Then recite 7 times, 11 times or 100 times rightafter:

Allahu hu, Malikun, Semi´un, Qadir´un (Kadirun), Kerim, Halim´un, Latief´un, Alim´un, Muin´un, Saadiq - Amin

You can also recite...

(first, do the prayer and ask Allah for a certain thing), then recite

1111 times Surah Al-Hijr, 95th ayat (verse)

"Innaa kefeynaakel mustehziin (mustehziine)

and then

7 times Ali-Imran Surah, 154th ayat (verse)

"Summe enzele aleykum min ba'dil gammi emeneten nuasen yagşa taifeten minkum, ve taifetun kad ehemmethum enfusuhum yezun-nune billahi gayrel hakkı zannel cahiliyyeh, yekulune hel lena minel emri min şey', kul innel emre kullehu lillah, yuhfune fi enfusihim ma la yubdune lek, yekulune lev kane lena minel emri şey'un ma kutilna hahuna, kul lev kuntum fi buyutikum le berezellezine kutibe aleyhimul katlu ila medaciihim, ve li yebteliyallahu ma fi sudurikum ve li yumahhısa ma fi kulubikum, vallahu alimun bi za-tis sudur"

Is said to be powerful

Recitation for „On the Go"

„La havle ve la kuvvete illa billahil aliyyil azim"

Recitation: 21 Mal,33 Mal, 1000 Mal

In this prayer we praise Allah and His power. The name of Allah „El-Azim" is hidden here. This prayer protects us from problems or helps us to overcome problems.

To recite Salatu-Selam (Salawat) regularly is mentioned in Quran: (el-Ahzâb, 56). The simplest form is:

„Essalâtuu vesselâmuu aleyke yâ Rasulallah"

recitation: 100 times or 1000 times

it is also possible to recite any of the 99 esma´s of Allah on the go (and anytime).

Reciting Ayat Al Kursi (Baqara surah verse 255) protects when travelling.

„Bismillahirrahmanirrahim"

„Allahu la ilahe illa huvel hayyul kayyum, la te'huzuhu sine-tun ve la nevm, lehu ma fis semavati ve ma fil ard, men-zellezi yeşfeu indehu illa bi iznih ya'lemu ma beyne eydihim ve ma halfehum, ve la yuhitune bi şey'in min ilmihi illa bi ma şae, vesia kursiyyuhus semavati vel ard, ve la yeuduhu hıfzuhuma ve huvel aliyyul azim."

Translation:

„in the name of Allah, the All-Merciful, the Merciful"

"there is no God but Allah, the living and the constant (the one without beginning and without end). He has neither slumber nor sleep. Allah is always awake and sees everything at all times. To Him belongs (everything) that is in the heavens and what is on earth, and He keeps alive everything that He has created. He holds everything (the universes and everything in them) firmly together.

Nobody could intercede with Him – except with His permission!

He knows what is before them and what is behind them (in time), but they (humans and everything else He has created) do not include anything of His knowledge – except what He wants them to know!

His power (dominion) encompasses the (all) heavens and the Earth, and their protection does not weigh Him down. He is the Exalted and All-Powerful.

Prayers for Forgiveness and Healing

Allah rewards us more highly and forgives us more readily when we recite the prayers that are rarely used today. The reward is especially high when we pass on prayers of this kind to others. This prayer can be repeated very well while you are on the road a lot and actually do not have time to recite.

„Lâilâhe illallâhuu vahdehû lâ şerîkeleh, lehu'l-mulku velehu'l-hamdu yuhyî ve yuumîtuu ve huve hayyun lâ-yemûtu bi-yedihi'l-hayri ve huve 'alâ kulli şey'in kadîr." (Tirmizî, Da'avât 36, 3424) can be recited on the go or in the city, in the park..it is said to have a high reward, when reciting on fresh air when other people are around.

Before falling asleep 3 times following prayer should help to achieve forgiveness from Allah.

"Estagfirullah el-azim ellezi lâ ilahe illâ huvel hayyel kayyume ve etubu ileyh" (Tirmizî)

The following prayer, which our prophet himself is said to have used regularly, promises healing and protects against health ailments:

„Bismillahirrahmanirrahim, Elhamdulillahillezi afani mimmebtelake bihi ve feddaleni ala kesirin mimmen haleka tafdila" (Tirmizi)

„Jahrucu min butunihee serabum muhtelifun elveenuhu fihi sifa ul linnasi" (Nahl Sure, 69.th ayat (verse))

„Fe Lemma elkav kale musa ma ci´tum bihis sihr (sihru), innallahe se yubtiluhu, innallahe la yuslihu amelel mufsidin (mufsidine)" (Yunus Sure, 81.th ayat (verse))

If we wish to ask Allah for forgiveness, we can recite the following ayat (verse) one time (or more) following the morning prayer:

En´am surah, 1. Ayat (Verse), 2. Ayat (Verse), 3. Ayat (Verse):

Bismillahirrahmanirrahim

1. Elhamduulillahillezî halagassemavâti vel arda vecealezzulumâti vennûr. Suummellezîne keferû birabbihim ya'dilûn

2. Huuvellezî halagakum min tıynin suumme gadâ ecelâ ve ecelummuusemmen indehû suumme entuum temterûn

3. Ve huuvallâhu fissemâvâti ve fil ard. Ya'lemu sirrakum ve cehrakum ve ya'lemu mâ teksibûn.

The Prayer of Hızır in Hıdırellez

The word Hıdırellez is supposed to have come from a combination of Hızır (Khidr) and İlyas (Elijah).

Who were these two men and how are they connected?

Hızır (which means Green Man in Arabic) has been tied to early Middle Eastern legends of spring, the renewal of warm weather among the Mesopotamians and the Egyptians, the reflowering of plants and the growth of new crops. Similar beliefs and celebrations were to be found among the various peoples of Anatolia and Central Asia. But the origin of Khidr or Hızır is obscure. His name is not mentioned in the Bible or in the Quran. There's no real explanation as to why this person is called the Green Man (Khidr) although some say it was because the Prophet Muhammad (sallallahu 'alayhi wa sallam, SAW, meaning: Peace be upon him))

wore a green cloak while others attribute it to his role in the greening of the earth in spring time.

One of the Islamic traditions, however, says that the Prophet Moses went to Ethiopia to acquire knowledge and, while there, he met a man named Khadir (Hızır). In the story, the two men have a fish which they intend to eat; however, they forget it and it gets away. It's possible that this was Hızır. The latter is supposed to have then tested Moses by insisting that he not ask the reason why he performed three acts.

But Moses was unable to understand the meaning of the actions and impatiently asked why each time, at which point the man refused to teach Moses because of his impatience (Quran, 18: 60-82). In the Quran (Chapters 37 and 6), Elijah is called Elias and he is mentioned several times in which he tries to persuade the people of Israel to continue to worship God, rather than false idols. He is also one of the prophets praised by God for being righteous. Hızır and Elijah have been described as "the two 'guardian spirits' of this world and the next."

Hızır is supposed to have drunk the water of life and achieved immortality. This made him one of the four immortals that included Idris, Jesus and Elijah. As an immortal, Hızır is believed to be able to grant people their wishes, distribute wealth and good fortune and restore health. For example, he is credited with giving the gift of poetry to the 14th-century Persian poet Hafiz and, according to tradition, Hızır not only served as the guide of Moses, but also of Alexander the Great.

According to a tradition (hadith) that is attributed to the Prophet Muhammad, Hızır and Elijah meet every year in Jerusalem, some say during the month of Ramadan and that they then perform the pilgrimage together. There they drink enough water from the well of Zamzam to tide them over for another year. They are also supposed to meet at Arafat, which is one of the places that are part of the rituals associated with the pilgrimage.

According to legend, Hizir had recited a special prayer, where he recites all of 99 Names of Allah and some more, which are mentioned in Quran. This prayer should be recited either three, five or seven times each prayer and promises to fulfill all desires, helps out from difficult situations and gives you inner balance.

The prayer of Hizir

Bismillahirrahmanirrahim

La ilahe illellahul hayyul kayyum

La ilahe illellahul bakid deymum

La ilahe illellahu vahdehu la sherike leh

La ilahe illellahul evvelul ahir

La ilahe illellahuz zahirul batin

La ilahe illellahul azizul cebbar

La ilahe illellahul hakimul gaffar

La ilahe illellahul semiy´ul basiyr

La ilahe illellahul latiyful habir

La ilahe illellahul gafurush shekur

La ilahe illellahul vehhabul kadir

La ilahe illellahul halimul alim

La ilahe illellahul cevadul kerim

La ilahe illellahlul berrur rahiym

La ilahe illellahul azizul hakiym

La ilahe illellahul hafidur rafiu

La ilahe illellahul hafiyzul mugniy

La ilahe illellahul kerimul mu´tiy

La ilahe illellahul kaimuz zeiyy

La ilahe illellahul aliyyul behiyy

La ilahe illellahush sheridur rakiyb

La ilahe illellahul karibul mucib

La ilahe illellahul fettahul aliym

La ilahe illellahul vekiylur rezzak

La ilahe illellahul metekebbirul halik

La ilahe illellahul evvelu min added

La ilahe illelahul bakiy bi gayri meded

La ilahe illelahul vedudul meciyd

La ilahe illellahul feálu lima yurid

La ilahe illellahul melikul varis

La ilahe illellahul bakil bais

La ilahe illellahul bariul musavvir

La ilahe illellahul latiyful mudebbir

La ilahe illelllahus seyyidud deyyan

La ilahe illellahul hannanul mennan

La ilahe illellahu zul fadliy vel ihsan

La ilahe illellahul hadil kaviyy

La ilahe illellahu zul ahdil vefiyy

La ilahe illellahul hakkul mubin

La ilahe illellahut tevvabul muiyn

La ilahe illellahul kebiru zul in´ami vel ihsani vel celal

La ilahe illellahu zul kerami vel ifdal

La ilahe illellahul ferdus samed

La ilahe illellahul leyse lehu sahibeten ve la veleda

La ilahe illellahul basitul bedi´yu

La ilahe illellahu zul hisabis seriy ´i

La ilahe illellahul vasiu zul ihsan

La ilahe illellahus selam´ul mumin

La ilahe illellahul kefiylul muheymin

La ilahe illellahul hakimul kerim

La ilahe illellahu rabbus semavati vel erdi ve rabbul arshil aziym

Ve sallellau ala seyyidina ve nebiyyina muhammedin ve alihi ve sahbihi ecmeiyn

Bi rahmetike ya erhamer rahimiyn

„Whoever contributes to the doing of good, he himself has performed the good (with Allah"

Tirmizî, İlim, 14

„In the name of Allah the All-Merciful, the Merciful"

„Verily, Allah was generous to the believers,

since He raised up among them a messenger from among you.

Who reads His verses to them and purifies them with them..."

(Surah Ali-Imran, verse 164)

The Intention

The importance of the intention in our heart during a recitation or the performance of a prayer influences the way it works.

„The deeds (of men) are according to their intentions, and every man (is due) what he intended."

[Sahih al-Buchari, Chapter 1/Hadithnr. 1]

Intention is crucial to the way the recitation and prayers work. We can ask for things in this world or for things in the hereafter as well as for forgiveness.

In the prayer „Rabbena Atina" we ask Allah for both, worldly things and a contented life in the hereafter. We should always strive for a healthy balance of both. Reciting without specific intentions is much more valuable with Allah and will be rewarded higher,

In schā' Allāh.

"I meet the positive expectations that My servant has of Me; and

I am with him (her) when he (she)   remembers Me:

If he(she) remembers Me in his (her) heart, I also remember him (her) among Myself.

If he (she) remembers Me in an assembly, I also remember him (her) in an assembly better than that.

If he (she) meets Me by a hand length, then I meet him (her) by an arm length.

If he (she) meets Me by an arm's length, I meet him (her) by two arm's lengths."

[Sahih Muslim, Hadithnr. 4832/chapter 48 Words of Allah]

128

Zeitfracht Medien GmbH
Ferdinand-Jühlke-Straße 7
99095 Erfurt, Deutschland
produktsicherheit@kolibri360.de